# Dolphin Life

# Funny & Weird

# Marine Mammals

**Funny & Weird Animals Series**

By

## P. T. Hersom

Dolphin Life Funny & Weird Marine Mammals

By P. T. Hersom

First Published, 2013

Printed in the United States of America

Hersom House Publishing

3365 NE 45th St, Suite 101

Ocala, Florida 34479 USA

This book is dedicated to my son Gabriel who loves to swim with the dolphins.

Love you Gabriel,

Daddy

# Dolphins are Marine Mammals

Marine mammals are animals that breathe air, live in the water, give live birth as opposed to laying eggs, nurse their young and are warm blooded. Dolphins, whales, seals, sea lions, porpoises, manatees, sea otters and even polar bears are marine mammals.

Dolphins have hair! What? Yes, every mammal has hair even marine mammals! For many marine mammals like seals, polar bears and sea lions, their hair creates a warm insulation to protect them from cold water and air. Dolphins, whales and porpoises only have hair on their faces and many lose their hair shortly after being born.

Many marine mammals have a thick layer of fat on their body called blubber, which stores energy and keeps them warm. Most spend their entire life in the water, but some spend more time on land. Dolphins, whales and manatees have to stay in the water. However, seals, walruses, otters and polar bears come out of the water to eat, lie in the sun, to mate and give birth.

Scientists group marine mammals into four different groups: Cetaceans, Pinnipeds, Sirenians and Fissipeds.

Cetaceans – consist of dolphins, whales and porpoises which completely spend their life in the water.

Pinnipeds – meaning fin-footed, such as walruses, sea lions and seals have four fins or flippers, two in the back and two in the front. They spend most of their time in the water, but go to land to breed.

Sirenians – also known as sea cows, like the manatee and dugong have two arms and a paddle shaped tail. They spend all their life in the water and never go to land.

Fissipeds – have separate digits, meaning fingers, thumbs and toes, such as the polar bear and otter. They spend most of their time on land and go to the water for food.

# Dolphin Life

Dolphins live in family groups called schools or pods ranging from 6 to 50 dolphins. Some pods though, can grow to more than 10,000 individuals. The daddy dolphin is called a bull, the mommy dolphin called a cow, and baby dolphins are called calves. Calves will nurse from their mother from 11 to 24 months before eating fish. They stay with their mother until at least 3 years old.

There are almost 40 different kinds of dolphins with many varied colors, shapes and sizes. Some dolphins are only 4 ft/1.2m long, while others grow to over 30 ft/9.5m in length. They breathe through a blowhole located on top of their head.

All dolphins are carnivores, which mean they are meat eaters and when it comes to eating, dolphins like fish, squid and crustaceans like shrimp. Dolphins do not chew their food, but swallow it whole! Larger dolphins such as the killer Whale will also eat other marine animals.

Dolphins have superb hearing and eyesight, and find food through echolocation. Echolocation is when the dolphin makes clicking sounds that travel underwater until they hit fish, then bounce back revealing the location, shape and size. Then the pod of dolphins will work together corralling a school of fish into a tight group, called a bait ball. Then take turns swimming through the ball, feeding on the fish.

Dolphins are intelligent social mammals that communicate with each other through vocal clicks and whistle sounds. They are known for their interactive and playful personalities. Often seen greeting ships coming and going from a harbor, by bow-riding and bow-wave surfing.  Truly the aerial acrobats of the sea, jumping high out of the water performing amazing stunts and winning the hearts of many visitors of marine themed parks. Dolphins love to interact with people both in captivity and in the wild.

When it's time for bed, dolphins sleep with one part of their brain awake and the other in slow-wave sleep mode. This allows them to stay awake just enough to watch for predators and keep their blowholes above water to breathe. Weird. Instead of sleep walking would you call this sleep swimming?

## Is a Porpoise a Dolphin?

No, a porpoise is not a dolphin, but they are part of the same marine mammal family as the whale and dolphin, called the cetaceans.

Porpoises are generally smaller and stouter than dolphins. They have triangular dorsal fins like sharks and flattened spade shaped teeth; where as the dolphin's teeth are pointed. Porpoises do not have beaks, but blunt jaws and round small heads. They are very shy and rarely seen jumping out of the water, near boats or people.

# Amazon River Dolphin

**Size:** Up to 8.2 ft/2.5m in length and weigh 215 lb/98 kg.

**Where they live:** In the Amazon and Orinoco River basins of South America.

**Tell Me More**

This funny looking pink colored dolphin, yes it is actually pink, live in the freshwaters of the Amazon and Orinoco rivers. Also known as the Boto or Pink Dolphin, these guys come in the light grey color pictured above or a carnation pink as shown in the photo below.

They have a unique ability to turn their heads 90 degrees which aids in navigating through the flooded rain forest areas of the river.

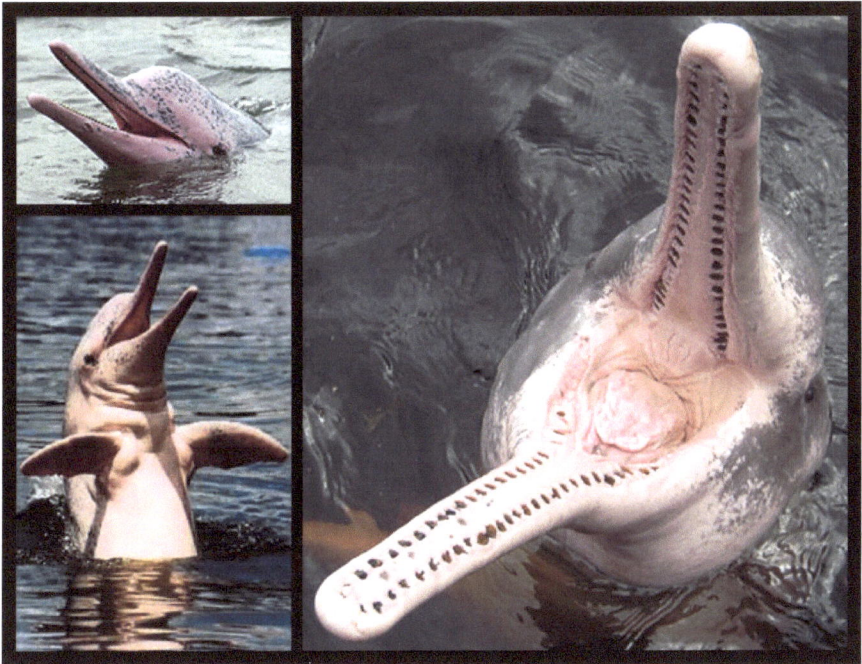

During the rainy season the river floods over its banks into forest and marsh areas. This is where the dolphin is well equipped; it hunts for prey through the underwater trees using its flexible neck and long snout to pull out fish from submerged vegetation.

Since this dolphin lives only in freshwater it gets to eat additional things not found in the saltwater oceans, such as *piranhas! Now that's truly taking a bite out of the river!*

# Atlantic Spotted Dolphin

**Size:** Up to 7.5 ft/2.25 m in length and weigh 300 lbs/136 kg.

**Where they live:** In the North Atlantic Ocean and the Gulf Stream.

**Tell Me More**

This spotted dolphin only gains its spots as it grows older. As dolphin calves, its color is mostly grey. When the dolphin calves are weaned off of its mother's milk and eating on its own, the spots start to appear. The upper part of their body is black or dark grey. The underneath belly is white. Dark spots will start to appear on this area and white spots on their upper dark area.

They are fast swimmers that like to bow-ride boats and are known for their playful airborne acrobatic displays. They talk to one another through whistles and loud clicks. *Click, click.*

# Bottlenose Dolphin

**Size:** Up to 13 ft/6.6 m and weigh 1,430 lbs/650 kg.

**Where they live:** In warm and tropical oceans worldwide.

**Tell Me More**

The Bottlenose Dolphin is the most recognized dolphin in the world. Known for its breaching ability, it can make high leaps of 16 ft/5 m into the air. They are popular stars in aquarium shows worldwide, and are known to have a high level of intelligence and easily trained. Even the military has used them to detect underwater mines and enemy divers.

Their charming personality is hard to resist, with their ever seemingly smile from their curved mouth and their playful eagerness to entertain.

They are friendly and interactive with people both in the wild and in captivity. They communicate by producing sounds from their blowhole, both whistles and squeaks. Have you ever made a squeak through your blowhole? No? Well maybe a whistle then?

# Commerson's Dolphin

**Size:** Up to 5 ft/1.5 m and weigh 55 lb/25 kg.

**Where they live:** Inlets of Argentina and the Strait of Magellan near the Falkland Islands.

**Tell Me More**

Also commonly called the Skunk Dolphin, Panda Dolphin and the Oreo Dolphin, just kidding about the "Oreo Dolphin", but if it was a cookie that's what it would be, the Commerson's distinctive coloring makes it easy to spot with the black fluke, dorsal fin and head, with the white creamy filling. I mean white body.

This dolphin is a fast swimmer and will swim behind speedy boats and bow-ride too. They are kind of show offs as they like to spin and twist while they swim, swim upside down and even surf on breaking waves near the beach. Funny, hang ten cookies.

# Common Dolphin

**Size:** Up to 8.5 ft/2.6 m and weigh 520 lb/236 kg.

**Where they live:** In warm and tropical oceans worldwide.

**Tell Me More**

The Common Dolphin is made of two types of dolphin, the Long-beaked and the Short-beaked Common Dolphin. Both species have the same coloring with the only difference being the length of their beaks. Though not widely recognized as the Bottlenose Dolphin, the Common Dolphin was the most seen in ancient literature and art of Rome and Greece.

Airborne acrobatics and breaching displays are common with this speedy swimmer. Speeds of up to 37 mph/60 km/h have been recorded. They like to gather in large pods of 100 to 1,000 dolphins, and some pods have been observed to have over 10,000 dolphins!

# Dusky Dolphin

**Size:** Up to 6 ft/1.8 m and weigh 210 lb/100 kg.

**Where they live:** In coastal waters of the Southern Hemisphere.

**Tell Me More**

Besides its unique coloring this small dolphin can easily be identified by its evenly sloped head and the lack of a beak at the end of its snout. They generally socialize within pods of 50 to 500 dolphins and are funny aerial tumblers.

They love to breach the water and do many different in air moves including head over tail flips, nose outs, head slaps, tail slaps and spins. Their communication consists of squeaks, squeals, clicks and whistles which can be heard up to 2 m/3.2 km away when they're out of the water.

# Hector's Dolphin

**Size:** Up to 5 ft/1.5 m in length and weigh 130 lb/60 kg.

**Where they live:** Only in the coastal waters of New Zealand.

**Tell Me More**

Named after the New Zealand scientist Sir James Hector, who discovered the species, the Hector Dolphin is the smallest dolphin in the world and also the rarest. On their torpedo shaped body they have a distinctive rounded dorsal fin and no beak on their snout. Socially they like to group into pods of 8 to 10 dolphins.

They are a slower swimmer and communicate with clicking sounds. They are the only dolphin that does NOT use whistling for communication. Scientists are still puzzled as to why they do not whistle. I guess maybe they never learned how, hum... funny.

# Hourglass Dolphin

**Size:** Up to 6 ft/1.8 m in length and weigh 260 lb/ 120 kg.

**Where they live:** In sub Antarctic and Antarctic Ocean waters.

**Tell Me More**

This dolphin gets its name from the two white patches on its side which is connected by a thin white strip, creating kind of an hourglass shape. They commonly are seen riding the bow waves of ships.

Since they share feeding grounds with many different types of whales, they were given the nickname "look outs" by whale hunters, which used them to help discover feeding whales.

# Killer Whale or Orca

**Size:** Up to 32 ft/9.7 m in length and weigh 12,000 lb/5,443 kg.

**Where they live:** In all oceans throughout the world.

**Tell Me More**

The killer Whale is the most powerful predator on earth and an apex predator, meaning it has no natural enemy. They are the largest member in the dolphin family and dive down to 1,000 ft/305 m when looking for food. That's a long way to hold your breath!

Like other dolphins they feed on fish, plus much larger prey like seals, sharks and whales. Hunting together in groups or packs similar to what wolfs do, they are sometimes called "The Wolves of the Sea".

Killer Whales are intelligent predators and are known for "spyhopping", which is when the whale holds its head above water and looks around for prey, such as penguins standing on top of ice floes. Working together several Killer Whales will form a line and swim swiftly towards the ice floes. A line of whales push a lot of water and just before impact they turn away and the water surges over the ice, backwashing the penguins into the sea.

Killer Whales have the second largest brain of any marine mammal. Being very social they use whistles, clicks and even a variety of screams to communicate with each other. Have you ever screamed to communicate with someone? Scientists have noticed that some pods even have their own language.

# Pacific White-sided Dolphin

**Size:** Up to 8ft/2.5 m in length and weigh 440 lb/200 kg.

**Where they live:** In cool waters of the North Pacific Ocean.

## Tell Me More

You may see these dolphins starring in a marine theme park show, a long side their cousin the Bottlenose Dolphin. The Pacific White-sided Dolphin is holding a pose in the picture above.

Socially they gather into pods of 10 to 100 individuals. These dolphins are really active and mix with other dolphin species. They are friendly and playful and are commonly seen approaching boats to bow-ride and perform acrobatics of somersaults and belly flops. Ouch!

# Pilot Whale

**Size:** Up to 24 ft/7.2 m in length and weigh 7,055 lb/3200 kg.

**Where they live:** In oceans worldwide.

**Tell Me More**

Pilot Whales are the second largest dolphin and are sometimes called blackfish due to their black coloring. They can dive to deep depths of 2,000 ft/610 m and hold their breath up to 16 minutes before coming back to the surface. They have been nicknamed Cheetahs of the Deep because of the fast swimming ability in deep water.

They have a high level of social activity and talk with different sounds such as whistles, squeals, clicks, snores and whining. I know some people talk by whining, but not by snoring? Now that's funny!

# Risso's Dolphin

**Size:** Up to 14 ft/ 4.3 m in length and weigh 1,100 lb/500 kg.

**Where they live:** Worldwide in tropical and temperate ocean waters.

**Tell Me More**

Risso's Dolphins usually gather in pods of 10 to 50 dolphins, though pods of up to 400 have been seen. They like to hang out in deeper waters feeding mainly on squid. If you look closely to the photo above you can see scars on the dolphin's skin from larger squid encounters.

Risso's Dolphins are shy and normally do not approach boats or bow-ride. I guess surfing is not in their blood.

# Southern Right Whale Dolphin

**Size:** Up to 9.5 ft/3 m in length and weigh 220 lb/100 kg.

**Where they live:** In cool temperate ocean waters of the Southern Hemisphere.

## Tell Me More

Southern Right Whale Dolphins are easily identified by their black and white coloring and the fact that they have no dorsal fin on their back. They are fast swimmers and have the most slender body of any dolphin. However, that does not keep them from having fun by breaching; belly flopping and slapping their flukes on the water surface.

These dolphins are commonly seen with other dolphins like the Hourglass, Dusky and Pilot Whale Dolphins.

# Spinner Dolphin

**Size:** Up to 7.5 ft/2.5 m in length and weigh 175 lb/79 kg.

**Where they live:** In tropical and subtropical ocean waters worldwide.

**Tell Me More**

Named for their high spinning leaps, spinner dolphins are known as playful and excited bow-riders. On the island of Hawaii, Spinner Dolphins not only come close to boats, but could be called "Ambassadors of Aloha." Native Hawaiian traditions deem dolphins to be an oceanic tribe with equal rights as islanders. They work together with them to fish to this day. Funny, but true.

# Striped Dolphin

**Size:** Up to 8.5 ft/2.6 m in length and weigh 350 lb/160 kg.

**Where they live:** In tropical and temperate ocean waters worldwide.

**Tell Me More**

The Striped Dolphin is one of the most abundant dolphins in the world and can easily be identified by its set of stripes that run down the side of its body. They are social and fast swimmers breaching the water up to 20 ft/6 m high into the air! They perform a special aerobatic trick called "roto-tailing" which is when they leap into the air and at the same time briskly rotate their tail. Can you jump and shake your tail at the same time?

# White-beaked Dolphin

**Size:** Up to 10ft/3 m in length and weigh 800 lb/363 kg.

**Where they live:** In the North Atlantic Ocean.

## Tell Me More

Named for its short thick white beak the White-beaked Dolphin is social and will often surf on the bow wave of boats. They usually gather into pods of 5 to 30 dolphins, but pods of 1,500 dolphins have been seen.

Known as social feeders they generally feed along side with Humpback, Killer and Fin Whales and other dolphin species too.

# Pink Bottlenose Dolphin

**Size:** About 6 ft/1.8 m in length.

**Where they live:** In Calcasieu Lake which is located in Louisiana, USA.

**Tell Me More**

"Pinky" was first discovered in 2008 by a charter boat captain on this inland saltwater lake off the Gulf of Mexico. Pinky is an albino Bottlenose Dolphin and not only has pink colored skin, but also has red eyes. Pinky has become a big splash with locals and tourists. In the photo above Pinky is seen swimming with his mother. Weird, huh?

# What Did You Learn Today? Questions

1. Pinky is an Amazon River Dolphin, true or false?
2. Can dolphins talk to each other with whistle and click sounds?
3. I'm usually the star attraction at marine theme parks? What is my name?
4. Do Commerson's Dolphins like to eat Oreo cookies?
5. Some pods of the Common Dolphin have numbered over 10,000, true or false?
6. The Dusky Dolphin is known as an aerial tumbler and can do head over tail flips, nose outs and spins, true or false?
7. The Hector's Dolphin is only found in the coastal waters of what country?
8. True or false, the Hourglass Dolphin is nicknamed "look outs" because they run over people swimming?
9. Do Killer Whales scream at each other?
10. The Pacific White-sided Dolphin likes to do belly flops, true or false?
11. My name is Pilot Whale and I can hold my breath for 16 minutes. Am I a whale or a dolphin?
12. The Risso's Dolphin may get scars on its sides from hunting swordfish, true or false?
13. Southern Right Whale Dolphins do not have a dorsal fin, true or false?

14. The Spinner Dolphins do high spinning leaps, true or false?

15. I can jump 20 ft/6 m into the air and do a roto-tail at the same time. What is my name?

16. The White-beaked Dolphin likes to eat insects like a bird, true or false?

17. Pinky the Bottlenose Dolphin has red eyes because he drank too much Louisiana Hot sauce, true or false?

# What Did You Learn Today? Answers

1) False, Pinky is an albino Bottlenose Dolphin.

2) Yes.

3) The Bottlenose Dolphin.

4) I don't know. I never wanted to share my Oreos, but they are colored like an Oreo cookie, black, white and black.

5) True.

6) True, and they also do head slaps and tail slaps.

7) New Zealand.

8) False, it's because hunting whalers use them to find feeding whales.

9) Yes!

10) True, and somersaults too.

11) A dolphin.

12) False, from hunting squid.

13) True, but all other dolphins do.

14) True.

15) The Striped Dolphin.

16) False.

17) False, it's because he is an albino dolphin.

# Other Books to Enjoy by P. T. Hersom

Click to LOOK INSIDE!

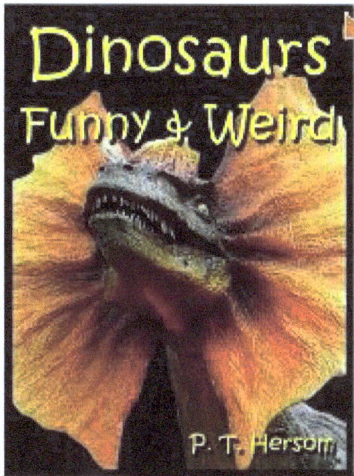

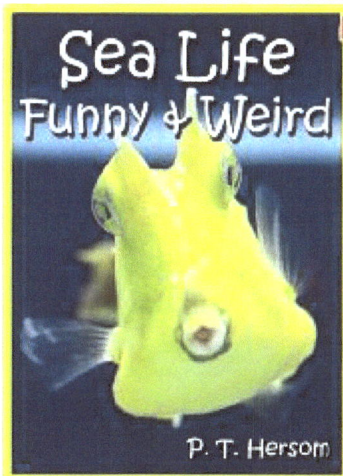

Dinosaurs Funny & Weird

P. T. Hersom

kindle edition

Click to LOOK INSIDE!

Sea Life Funny & Weird

P. T. Hersom

kindle edition

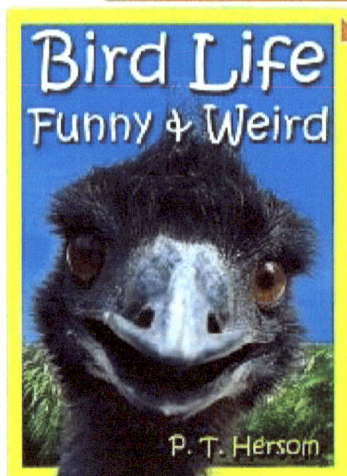

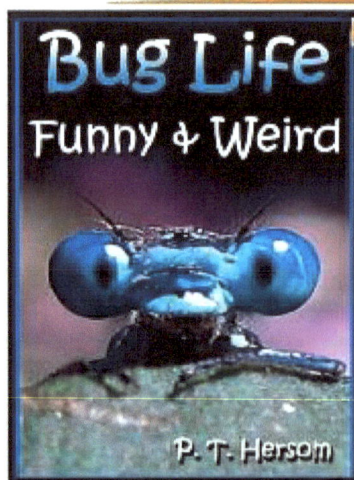

# Bird Life
## Funny & Weird

P. T. Hersom

# Bug Life
## Funny & Weird

P. T. Hersom

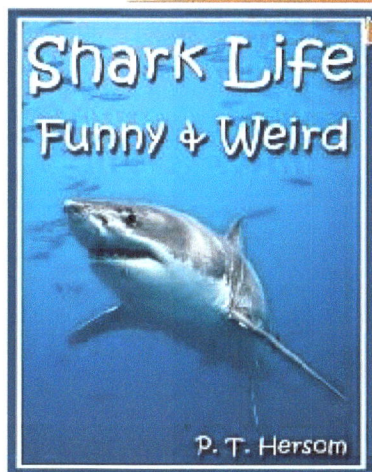

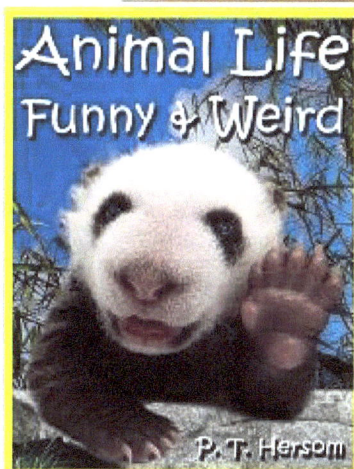

# Shark Life
## Funny & Weird

P. T. Hersom

kindle edition

# Animal Life
## Funny & Weird

P. T. Hersom

kindle edition

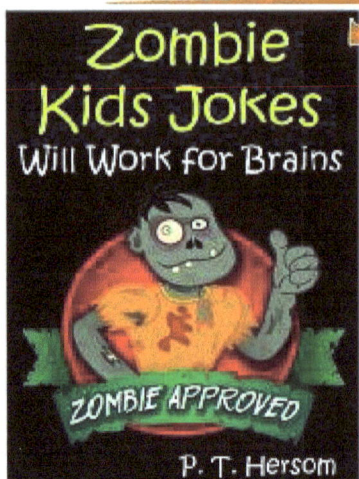

Click to **LOOK INSIDE!**

Zombie
Kids Jokes
Will Work for Brains

ZOMBIE APPROVED

P. T. Hersom

kindle edition

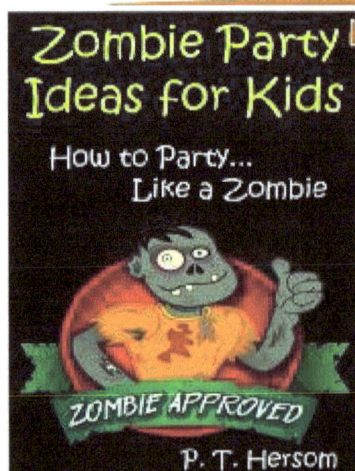

Click to **LOOK INSIDE!**

Zombie Party
Ideas for Kids

How to Party...
Like a Zombie

ZOMBIE APPROVED

P. T. Hersom

kindle edition

## Enjoyed the Book?

Thank you for buying this book. I hope that you and your children enjoy reading the book and learning about the animals in the book as much as I did writing it. If you found the book enjoyable, please help me out by posting a review on the Amazon page. Thank you for taking the time to do so. It is very much appreciated.

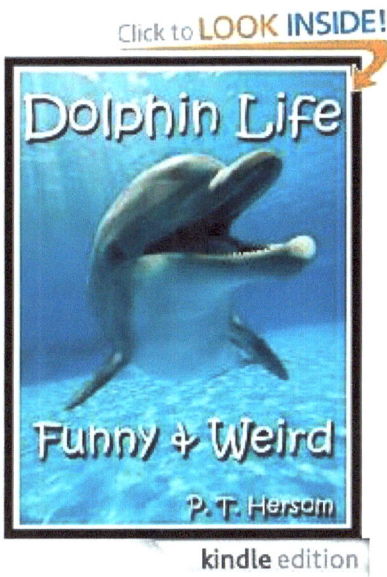

www.ingramcontent.com/pod-product-compliance
Lightning Source LLC
Chambersburg PA
CBHW041359090426

42741CB00001B/20